MW00915536

Swinging For Couples Vol. 2

The Intermediate Guide To The Swinging Lifestyle - 11 Things You Must Know To Ensure A Safe, Fun, Exciting, & Adventurous Swinging Experience

Natalie Robinson

Swinging For Couples Vol. 2

Publisher: Enlightened Publishing

ISBN-13: 978-1518708299

ISBN-10: 1518708293

Disclaimer

The Publisher has strived to be as accurate and complete as possible in the creation of this book. While all attempts have been made to verify information provided in this publication, the Publisher assumes no responsibility for errors, omissions, or contrary interpretation of the subject matter herein. Any perceived slights of specific persons, peoples, or organizations are unintentional.

This book is not intended for use as a source of legal, business, accounting or financial advice. All readers are advised to seek services of competent professionals in the legal, business, accounting, and finance fields.

The information in this book is not intended or implied to be a substitute for professional medical advice, diagnosis or treatment. All content contained in this book is for general information purposes only. Always consult your healthcare provider before carrying on any health program.

Table of Contents

Introduction

Welcome to Volume 2 of the Swinging For Couples series. This is the intermediate level guide and the continuation from my first book: "*Swinging For Couples Vol. 1: Beginner's Guide To The Swinging Lifestyle - 25 Things You Must Know Before Becoming A Swinger.*" In this book, we will cover the more advanced parts of swinging.

If you are completely new to the swinging lifestyle and have not yet read Volume 1, it is highly recommended that you take the time to read through the first guide, as it explains the fundamentals of swinging and contains many important definitions and terms which are helpful to have a full understanding of discovering the lifestyle and reading through this book.

Swinging is about trust, and trust is won through careful attention to rules, paying attention to boundaries, and not causing drama.

It is important to understand that swinging is not about having sex with anyone you feel like having sex with. It is not about cheating on your spouse or partner. It is, as I said, primarily about trust.

Most swingers will say that their relationships are stronger because of swinging. Swinging brought back that feeling they had when they were first with their spouse or partner, that excitement and anticipation they felt during the first date. One aspect of swinging that most people may find hard to believe is that seeing other people interested in and desiring your partner can actually make you desire them more.

There is, of course, nervousness during your first few swaps. The idea of swinging is an exciting one, but it can also be extremely nerve-wracking. Here is a scenario to consider: You are at your first gathering with your wife in tow, who is also very interested in swinging. You know your wife is hot; however, you also think you are hot. As the night wears on, she is getting more attention than you are. Men and women are gathering around her as you are both circulating, but you are not getting as much attention as she is.

At this point, you can choose one of two options: you can be jealous or you can revel in the fact that others also find your wife as attractive as you do. To truly swing, the second option is the one you need to take. You need to know how to tamp down your jealousy monster when it rears its head. You also need to know how to communicate your feelings to your wife. This book will cover how to do that in part. It will give ideas on how to get past the emotional upheaval that is bound to happen at certain times in your life.

At the end of the night, when you have completed your first swinging adventure, it is important, as well, to remember that swinging is supposed to be fun. If you did not have fun, felt too much jealousy and fear, or thought worse of yourself or your wife afterwards, then you should sit down and talk with your partner and decide if the decision to swing is the right one for you at that time. You may not be ready for it, emotionally. When you are ready for it, you will find that it is not only fun, but it is also bringing you and your partner closer together.

Even if you have already discovered a club you and your partner want to be a part of, or a couple you and your partner are going to swing with, there is still a lot to learn about the swinging lifestyle.

In this guide, you'll learn the importance of your reputation, of hygiene and ethics to those in the swinging world, how to host the other couple at your own venue, how to swing discreetly, how to play rough but safe, and you will also get a peek at some of the different fetishes you may or may not come across during your journey.

Ready? Let's get started!

Chapter 1: The Importance of Reputation

Reputation is an important aspect of successfully engaging in the swinging lifestyle. Your reputation can proceed you, and remain behind you long after you and your partner are gone, so it is important that the two of you pay attention to the relationships you are making, the way you are treating the other couples around you and the respect that you give to those that you play with, as well as those that you don't choose to engage with.

So how do the two of you make sure that you are establishing a good reputation for yourselves? A good rule of thumb for keeping your reputation golden is to respect others' preferences, the rules of the clubs and online sites, and practice good ethics both publicly and privately. Treat the person with whom you are swapping with the same respect you want your partner to receive from others.

Do not touch a woman's breasts or fondle her in the social area of the party, especially if you are just trying to warm her up or think you are flirting with her. Contrary to popular belief, most women do not like their nipples fondled unless they are already horny. It is not only annoying, but it also carries with it a "rapey" vibe.

The same is true for women. Flirt! Flirting is fun, and it will help you decide upon whether you want to be with the person or not. Rubbing a guy's cock out of nowhere, though, that is disrespectful and not actual flirting. He may not be as into you as you are into him, and now you have touched his penis, even if it is through his pants, and made him feel uncomfortable. Do not be that person. That person does not get invited to play, does not get invited to parties, and does not make a lot of friends.

While every swinger organization is different, most of them allow the members to pick and choose from the group whom they wish to sleep with. What a good group will not do is to force, require, or expect the members to play or have sex with anyone that they are not comfortable engaging with. However, that should not keep you from politely speaking to the couples that you are not interested in playing with, as it would not only come across as rude, but it might eventually lead to you and your partner not being invited to events.

Establish a good reputation by always being on time and showing up when and where you say you will. Respond to all invitations, even if you are not going to attend the event. This will to ensure that the host and hostess know how many people to expect and prepare for.

Always be generous when you arrive at a party or event. Bring a gift for the host and hostess or even going one step further to see if there is anything you can help with. If you are at a club, and not a private party, be sure to tip the bartender generously with each order.

When you are in bed with another couple, always follow their rules as well as the rules that you and your partner have established for yourselves. Never be pushy or aggressive just to get another couple to sleep with you, and allow things to develop naturally, at their own pace.

Do not discuss any of your interactions with other couples in a negative light, nor reveal too much detail, unless the other couple is there with you, happily sharing the story.

What happens in a swingers encounter or event should stay at a swingers encounter and event.

Finally, be sure that you always clean up after yourselves. One of the worst things you can do for your reputation, besides talking indiscreetly about your trysts, is being known for being a sexual slob. Nothing is more unappetizing than having to clean up after other people's sexual encounters. So unless it is made clear before-hand that you do not have to clean up, always tidy after yourselves so that you are wanted back at the next event.

Reputation is not only important to individuals and couples, but it is an important thing to look for in clubs, groups, and online. The swinging lifestyle is comprised of a small percentage of the population and reputation is relied upon heavily. For instance, if an online site has a bad reputation for not policing their members very well, then people will stop coming to the site to find gatherings or play dates.

Imagine you are a member of an online site where you can look for people who are interested in swinging, but every person you contact turns out to be a scammer of some sort. They are out there and there are ways to spot them, but it would get really old, really fast. You would probably move on to another site at that point, one that has a better reputation within the community. The same is true for on- and off-site clubs.

If you went to an on-site club that had no rules at all, people did not respect your preferences, and it was filthy, you would not return. You would not be the only one, either. As the talk ran its way through the grapevine, other swingers would stop coming to that club as well.

Chapter 2: Practicing Good Hygiene

Good hygiene is not just about making sure you shower and shave before a party. It is about preventing the spread of disease as well. When you have any type of open sore, you are inviting bacteria to move in and play house. That is how infections start.

Because sex is often rough, and the skin of our genital areas are very sensitive and easily torn, it is very important to make sure you clean up both before you play and after each partner you have. Here is a list of a few things you can do to lessen the chance of receiving an infection or starting one.

- **Shower before you swap.**

    Even if you have showered before you left the house, if possible, shower when you are at the party as well, at the least, clean your genital area after you are finished with each partner.

- **Men: If you are not circumcised, make sure you clean under your foreskin**.

Smegma is gross tasting and smelling, and no one likes to get pubic hair and wet fuzz balls in their mouths. If you have gunk hanging out down there, no one will want to get with you.

- **Men: Shave at least an hour before the party.**

While a five o'clock shadow is attractive, it can cause abrasions in certain areas, which not only hurt, but also invite bacteria to take up residence. If you have one of those beards that grow quickly, bring shaving cream and a razor or two with you to the party. Excuse yourself from time to time and get a fresh shave in. Nothing hurts more than a beard burn in the nether regions.

- **Bring mouthwash with you.**

Use it after an encounter and before a new one. Use it after you smoke or eat.

Bring a toothbrush with you and give your teeth a quick brushing whenever you can. Minty fresh breath is a lot more attractive than semen-smelling breath or a mouth that tastes like an ashtray.

- **Clean yourself after each encounter.**

  Clean your genitals, your hands, and your face. If you have a beard, wash it. Make sure you clean under your fingernails as well. Do not touch another person's genitals directly after an encounter without washing your hands first. This will cut down on the amount of bacteria being transferred.

- **Keep your nails cut, cleaned, and filed. Get rid of any jagged edges.**

  Imagine you are with another woman. You start touching her softly, stroking her tender, wet pussy. She asks you to touch her inside. So you start to masturbate her. Your nails are jagged or very long. Perhaps they are a bit sharp. She may not notice that you are scratching her up inside yet, but she will. Any bit of bacteria that is introduced into her vagina will now find its way into her system. She has been compromised because you did not take the time to clean your hands and trim your nails before you entered her.

- **Do not wear giant rings or chunky jewelry.**

  Get rid of anything that can harm another person in anyway. Big rings can cause a lot of damage to the tender areas on a person's body. Necklaces can become choking hazards, or if you are on top, they can dangle in someone's face and eyes and become an annoyance. Jewelry can also carry bacteria that you do not want to introduce

- **Get tested for STIs and for AIDS.**

  This never hurts to do anyway, and you can feel safe in knowing that you will not get anyone sick. Even if you use condoms, checking for these diseases on a regular basis is a great idea. Condoms do not always prevent pregnancy or disease. Condoms break, rip, and shred. Using a condom does not guarantee you will not get a sexually transmitted infection (STI). Knowing you and the person you are with do not have an STI will prevent you from getting them.

- **Wash sex toys before you use them.**

  Do I need to give an example? Using dirty sex toys on someone is not only gross, but grossly negligent behavior. You may as well just throw some dirt and grime in there while you are it.

- **Women: Wipe after a bowel movement from the front to the back.**

  Wiping from the back to the front can introduce harmful bacteria into your vagina. You can get bacterial vaginosis, yeast infections, or urinary tract infections.

- **Women: If you must douche, use plain water only.**

  Douching is not as hygienic as you have been led to believe; however, women who swing may find that they get a lot of yeast infections, even if they clean up after every encounter.

I usually do not recommend douching at all, because douching will not rid your body of the semen that is already traveling toward the eggs, but douching with plain water will clean the semen out up to your cervix. If you douche with a vinegar solution, it will dry you out and get rid of all the happy, healthy bacteria that lives there, which invites other not-so-friendly bacteria to move in instead.

Vaginas hold a lot of semen inside. It is how they are made. A woman can get pregnant up to five days after someone ejaculated inside her if she ovulates— that is how long semen lives inside their body, looking for a prime target.

However, I have read from other swingers that douching with plain water has dropped the amount of times they have gotten yeast infections to practically nothing, while before they got them after every encounter.

If you follow these guidelines, and ensure that everyone you swing with also follows these guidelines, then you will find the incidence of infections to be limited to non-existent.

Chapter 3: Practicing Good Ethics

Ethics is the province of that which is in doubt. Much like philosophy, the ethics of any situation depends upon the population itself. What rules or preferences does the population hold dear? It is always important, whenever you are in a new or different culture, to familiarize yourself with the ethics of the group and try to follow them. For instance, I have heard that it is considered beyond rude to blow your nose in certain situations in Japan. Therefore, whilst visiting Japan, I would excuse myself before blowing my nose in those situations. It is the polite thing to do.

Ethics within the swinging lifestyle are just as important as reputation, and the two go hand in hand. Having good ethics will help to ensure you maintain a good reputation. While there are many rules within the swinging lifestyle related to respect, discretion, and boundaries, it is up to us to use our ethics to know how to behave in certain situations. Swingers are humans too, and do make mistakes. How you handle these situations, and how you apply your sense of ethics are very important.

Let's say that you and your partner are in a nightclub, and an overly intoxicated woman comes over and begins to interact with the female half of your couple. Both are into each other but it is increasingly clear that she has had too much to drink and her partner is nowhere to be found.

She is upping the ante on the situation and proceeding to be more and more physical with your partner, obviously wanting to do more than just lightly kiss and tease. She begins to work her hands over both of you, making it clear that she is ready for playtime. You are both attracted to her but she is so drunk that it is impossible to have a conversation about her other partner or boundaries.

There are a few choices that you can make. The first and easiest choice is to take advantage of the woman who wants to be taken advantage of.

The second is to try and find her partner or other half and to return her to him.

The third option is to find the host of the party or security from the nightclub and let them know about the overly intoxicated woman. Any good club or party hosts will immediately take charge of the situation, remove the overly intoxicated person from general public interaction, find her partner, and help them to get home safely.

As a couple, you could choose option number one. However, dire consequences can result from this decision, creating bad situations like an angry, unknowing partner or (even worse) the woman could wake up in bed with no memory of agreeing to engage in sex with you and your partner.

Choice number two, while noble, would be much better off handled by the people who know the attendees of the party, as they are much more equipped to handle both the drunk lady and the reunion between she and her partner, as well as getting her out of the party so she can't cause any further damage to her relationship or her own reputation.

Choice number three is the ethical choice to make, as it ensures the best outcome for all parties involved, leaving you as a couple with a solid reputation.

Another example of good ethics within the swinging community is that of being discreet. Let's say the two of you are at a party and have just finished playing with a nice couple privately. Suppose the other couple has an odd fetish or quirk, or that the woman has a botched breast implant job that makes her nipples stick out funny. Obviously you are not going to make uncomfortable remarks to the other couple while you are playing. Once you have returned to the party and are now mingling with other couples, suppose a gossipy woman comes up who has had a play date with the same couple in the past. She begins to say something derogatory about them to strike up a conversation. Something to the tune of, "Did you get the toe thing too?" or "Nice boob job, huh?"

Once again you have multiple options as far as how to respond in such situations. You can opt to respond back with your true feelings about the horrible boob job or the weird toe thing, allowing a gossipy and rude conversation to follow about the other couple.

You can opt to say something like," I'm not sure what you are talking about" in order to avoid the situation.

Or you can simply let the person know that you had a wonderful time with the other couple and don't have anything negative to say about them and then change the topic of the conversation.

While the first option might be the easiest and somewhat satisfying, it is ultimately the most destructive in the long run. Discretion is valued within the swinging community, as is being kind and respectful. Do not involve yourself in gossipy behavior. It will only hurt the two of you in the long run.

Public

Practicing good ethics while in public is a no-brainer. Not everyone wants their business aired. They do not want to ruin their reputation to those who are not part of the lifestyle, so do not do it for them. Keep what you and your partner do with other people to yourself unless otherwise specified by the other couple.

It can often be tempting to brag about the amazing threesome or foursome that you had the weekend before. Obviously it is extremely unethical to discuss any of these activities at your work place or with your friends that are not involved in the swinger lifestyle. Even if they might not pass judgment on you or your partner, you do not want to risk that what you tell them about who you were with or what you were doing will make it around to other (non-swinger) social circles.

Indiscretion can be damaging to not only your reputation, but also to the reputation of the other couples as well, possibly causing them to lose their job or "normal" friends, or even causing family rifts should their kids, parents, or other family members find out.

For instance, you do not want to post on Facebook, "Jillian just sucked my dick so good!" Jillian's family, friends, and co-workers may not know about her lifestyle, and furthermore, she may not want them to know.

Another form of public ethics is to conform to the set of rules at any party or gathering that you attend. This is, essentially, the easiest thing for you and your partner to do. Find out the rules before you attend and follow them. Always remember that if you are going to a private party, you are more than likely going into someone's actual place of residence. Treat their property better than you would treat your own.

Here is a list of general rules to follow when attending a party:

- Dress or undress appropriately. If you are going to be eating, stay dressed for hygiene reasons. After the dinner, the hosts may have a dress-down period, so that no one is completely dressed and everyone is comfortable. If this is the case, make sure you bring some kinky or sexy attire to change into.

- Arrive in the time frame given for arrival. It is not fashionable to be late. It is rude. You may also miss out on some fun if you arrive late, and no one likes that.

- Bring money to donate to the hosts of the party; they may not take it, but if it is a party that has a nice dinner and good drinks, those things cost money. If the party is thrown as part of a club function, you may have already paid your dues, but it never hurts to offer compensation to your gracious hosts.

- Bring food if the dinner is a potluck. Even if you do not cook it yourself, not bringing food to a potluck is just a jerk thing to do.

- Be part of the meet and greet. Some parties have a set time in which all people in attendance will gather around and introduce themselves. This is a good chance to get you and your couple the attention you want and to find the people who you want that attention from.

- Bring your "party" bag. This should include personal items such as toiletries, your dress-down clothes, bath towels, and wet wipes. You may also want to bring toys, lubricants, and condoms. While the hosts may supply some of these items, it is just polite to bring your own. Most parties have an area set aside for you to store your personal belongings, so you are not holding on to a bag all night, or taking up room in one of the play rooms with your junk.

- Make a drink if a bar is available, and be sure you know where to put your dirty glasses or throw away your plastic cups. Do not drink to excess though. Most swinger's clubs from on drunkards, so it is always best to limit your alcohol intake.

- Pick up after yourself.

- Wear a name tag if everyone else is wearing a name tag. This will help you meet people without constantly telling everyone your name or asking for theirs anyway.

- RSVP to party invitations. Hosts need to know how many people are going to be there. Do not show up if you did not RSVP.

- Exchange phone numbers if you honestly want to set up a date with that person/couple, but do not exchange phone numbers just to be polite. If someone gives you their number, take it and thank them, but do not feel like you have to reciprocate. If you give someone your number, you are telling them to call you or text you and they will. Sometimes repeatedly. If you have been the person calling and are always told that this weekend is not going to work, take the hint—they are no longer interested.

- Leave your camera at home and your cell phone on vibrate. Most clubs and parties do not allow pictures for various reasons. So just do not take any.

- Gossip about your friends and family if you must, but not about other swingers. Gossip travels quickly, and it can ruin your reputation and theirs. Do not take it upon yourself to do that. If you have a problem with what someone is doing, bring it up to the host and ask for their advice, if you must. If it does not affect you or your partner, though, leave it alone.

- Ask someone to play with you. If you feel like you are not sparking someone's attention, it may not be because you are not attractive to them, it may be because they are shy or new to the lifestyle. The worst they can say is, "No, thank you, but thanks for asking."

Private

Practicing ethics in private may be a bit harder for some people. Most clubs have a set of rules that they ask you to follow, and most couples or swingers have a set of preferences they want you to follow. Here are a few things to remember when you enter into the swinging lifestyle:

- Say, "No, thank you, but thanks for asking," when you do not want to play with someone. Be polite.

- Be understanding. If someone says no thank you, do not push them to tell you why. You may not want to hear why. It may have nothing at all to do with you. Just say thank you and walk away.

- Remember the rules that no means no. If someone says no to you, thank them for their time, and move on. If the girl you are playing with says, "No, that does not feel good," do not keep doing whatever you are doing. Find something else to do with her and ask her if that feels better.

- Listen to your play partner, learn what they like and do not like.

- Play when you are healthy, not when you are infectious. If you have anything that another person can catch, not just STDs. You can attend a party for the social aspect of it, if you want, but decline any and all sexual activity until you are no longer infectious.

- Let people know if you are on your period. There are ways around it—wear your panties to show you are interested in that area right now, for instance—but if you do not mind having sex while you are on your period, make sure you let others know you are, because they may mind. If you do have sex while on your period, make sure you bring a good amount of towels with you. No host wants to take off bloody sheets the next morning.

- Set up your preferences and boundaries with your partner before you attend. Have clear signals that are not necessarily easy for others to interpret. This works for private parties, small gatherings, all the way through to a three-some. Knowing what you want and do not want beforehand can help you and your partner avoid many misunder-standings and help you have a good, fun time.

- Know which rooms in a party are private and which are not. If it is a private room and people are in it, do not go in there.

- Set an end time. This may not be an actual hour to go home, but a signal that says, "I'm done for the night, let's go." Both partners should leave at that time. If, however, one of you is still in a private room or is not finished with their current partner, be polite and wait until they are finished. Do not just rush into the room and drag your partner home. That is rude not only to him or her, but to the person or people they were with. You not only jeopardize your own relationship, but also the relationship with the other swingers in the group. That other person could not help but feel like they did something wrong, when in actuality, you are the one to blame. Another angle here is that if your partner tells you they want to go and you are not with someone, do not suddenly disappear to play with someone else.

- Find out if the other person wants to use a condom or not before you enter the bedroom. Do not wait until you are ready for insertion before bringing it up. Some people prefer bare-backing, some are allergy to latex and need a special brand, and some will never have sex with someone who is not their partner if a condom isn't used.

The most important part of private ethics is to remember that swinging is not cheating. If you do not have your partner's consent to have sex with someone else, no matter how much you wish to do it, do not.

Here is a situation I have seen before: A man, his wife, and another woman have a threesome. They have a great time. They follow rules and all three enjoy it. However, the other woman has a husband at home who has no idea what is happening. Later, the husband that was part of the threesome, gets together with the other woman, they have sex repeatedly, the whole while claiming they are swinging, but both spouses are now at home with no idea of what is going on with the other wife and husband. This is not swinging. This is cheating. Swinging is about open communication and honesty. It is about building trust between everyone involved. It isn't about having sex whenever you want with whomever you want.

Another important thing to remember is that sometimes emotions can run wild. If you find yourself in a situation where you suddenly feel overwhelmed by your emotions, try to find your partner and calmly let them know you need to talk with them. If you are interrupted by your partner in the middle of an act, calmly let the other person know you have to go talk with your partner. Do not put him or her off as that can make things worse. If you can't find your partner or you do not want to interrupt their play, find an unattached person or the host, and talk to them. Strangers usually listen pretty well and can help you clear your head in these situations.

If your partner isn't comfortable with you going with a certain person, listen to them. Your primary concern is your relationship with your partner, not with your orgasm. If they do not feel right about it, find out why.

Sit down and talk about it. Have a frank, open discussion. Perhaps it is because you have been playing with that person every time you go to a party. Doing so can result in infatuation and can quickly make a fun thing turn ugly. It may be hard, because you were having fun and really enjoying yourself with that guy, but if your partner feels uncomfortable, it is probably because he knows you well and knows that you are starting to fall for this other guy before you know it yourself. Going with the same person repeatedly can often result in hurt feelings on all sides.

This leads me into jealousy. He may feel uncomfortable because he can feel you falling in love, but he may also feel uncomfortable because he is starting to feel jealous of the attention you are giving this man. It is the easiest thing in the world to say, "Do not be jealous;" however, jealousy isn't something you can control. It can grab hold of you at the most inappropriate times.

The best way to try to curb your natural jealous tendencies is to ensure you and your partner have your boundaries and preferences mapped out before you start on your sexual journey. The key to controlling your jealousy is communication with your partner.

If you are not comfortable with your partner having sexual intercourse with another person at first, let them know. During your first couple of parties, take it slow. Perhaps, if your wife is bi-curious or bi-sexual, let her find a girl to play with that is ok with you watching.

You can try a soft swap, which does not involve penetration. There are various levels to the soft swap:

1. Kissing and playing on top of the clothing, usually the upper body only.

2. Still kissing and playing, but this level allows you to go under the clothing as well, but usually only the upper portion of the body.

3. Same as the second level, but you can stroke the lower portion of the body as well.

4. Playing and stroking with partial nudity.

5. All play mates are completely naked.

6. Kissing, playing, stroking, and oral sex.

Some people are fine with a full swap as long as their partner does not kiss the other person. If this is true for you, make sure your partner knows and agrees with it.

Start out slowly. If you feel jealousy when your partner is with someone else, try to figure out why you are feeling jealous. Look at your partner, see how much fun she is having; try to enjoy her natural desires and her excitement.

If you simply cannot get over it after the first time, and you do not think you ever will, then the lifestyle may not be for you or you may not be emotionally prepared for it. Take it slow and be sure you are ready if you try it again.

Maintain a high level of ethics both in the bedroom and outside of it. Have a sense of taking care of your fellow "brother" or "sister" swinger.

Even if you are not into them sexually, be sure to be good and kind to them. Often swingers groups are very close knit and look out for each other and help in different areas of one another's life.

In bed, be sure that you pay attention to and care for the sexual satisfaction and fantasies of the others with whom you are playing.

Do what you can to accommodate and please them sexually or to maintain a comfortable flow of play and interaction. This will help you establish a good rapport both in and out of the bedroom.

Chapter 4: Hosting and Guesting

Hosting a swinger's party isn't for everyone, but if you do decide to host a party, you will find some ideas below. It is important to plan on every eventuality you can. There are also some hard rules you cannot overlook.

Hosting a Party

Hosting a party requires more than hosting a couple does. It takes more time, more planning, and more money.

- Host your party at your house, or if you can afford it, host it in a hotel room.

- Know who you are going to invite. In other words, do not hold an open invitation party, as you may get guests who are not in the lifestyle, but want to come to a crazy sex party. These people do not know the rules of the lifestyle and can make others very uncomfortable.

- Make sure you give a solid date for RSVPs. Whenever I throw a party, I count how many people RSVP'd and add five. Once I hit that number, I turn away guests if they did not RSVP.

- Have a hard time when you will no longer answer the door. If you tell them you will not accept late arrivals after 8:00 pm, stick with it. You can make exceptions if a couple calls well in advance—like perhaps they do not get off of work until 9:00 pm. However, it is best if you pick a time and stick to it. Post a sign on the door that lets late guests know that they are too late.

- Make sure everyone knows that people are fully clothed when going through the food line if you are having food. It is far more hygienic that way.

- Ask for donations discretely; let your guests know where they can leave their donations and leave it at that. For instance, you can place a mason jar near the entry way with a small sign on it. Remember, though, that you may not be able to ask for payment, because you are not a licensed business. If you have a set donation in mind, let your guests know.

- Ask people to limit their alcohol intake. Do not allow people to get drunk or do drugs at your party. In most states, you are responsible for your guests' inebriation. If someone leaves your party drunk and drives, you could be liable. If a hotel guest smells weed, and you do not live in a state in which weed is legal, you could go to jail.

- Make sure that your home is clean and that all beds have clean sheets and fresh pillow cases and linens. Have reserves on hand should you need to change the beds to sleep.

- Have enough cleansing items for all of your guests, even if they are asked to bring their own. This will help if anyone forgets theirs, or if they did not bring enough of something.

- Make sure you decide upon what type of party it will be.

  1. **How old are the participants?** A lot of swingers have found that if they invite a plethora of ages, then some people will feel left out. For instance, if you have older men and younger women, the older men will ask the younger women, who may not be into having sex with older men. The women who are the ages of the older men will find themselves not being asked and feel left out, while the younger women may become turned off and want to leave.

  2. **Will it be full swap or soft swap?** Full swap parties get going faster while soft swap parties are slower in starting. Also, your guests, if the two types are mixed, will have to ask each person they meet which type of swinger they are. Mixing the types may make the party's tempo go even slower, and it may leave a few people empty handed at the end of the night.

- Make sure you have clearly marked play areas so people know where they can go. Have a few private rooms, an open play room, and a social area, at the least. Also, make sure there is enough room for the number of guests attending.

- Remember that a swinger's party is not like a normal party—the setting should exude sexuality. People who attend your party should feel the sexy vibes.

- Provide condoms, even if you have asked people to bring their own. They may have forgotten or not brought enough for the evening. Having them available to your guests will help people continue the sex play until the party winds down.

- Run the party like an orchestra and you are its maestro. Plan games that you can play – sexy games – throughout the night. Games that ramp up the sexual tension of the room and help the night along.

- Ensure that all of your guests know your rules for swinging. If everyone is playing by the same rules, then misunderstandings can be limited.

- Have a dress down area. A place for party-goers to change out of their party clothes and get comfortable and ready for sexual pleasure.

- Set aside an area for your guests to place their bags and belongings.

Hosting a Couple

Hosting a couple is a lot like hosting a party. You need to be sure they are into the same type of swinging you are. For instance, it probably would not go over too well if you wanted a full swap and invited a soft swap couple. You would not feel satisfied or satiated at the end of the evening.

However, if you are a full swap couple and do host a soft swap couple, you may find that you like the change. It may also be that you are in a position to mentor a new couple in the lifestyle. This couple may not be ready for full swap, but are interested in it. Perhaps, after a few soft swaps with that couple, they would like to learn more about a full swap or participate in one.

- If you are having the other couple over for dinner be sure to check if they have food allergies before deciding on your menu. Go one step further to ensure that they like what you are serving for dinner. Serving aphrodisiacs and having a small selection of wine, beer, or liquor are nice touches as well. If you can't afford to have all of these items on hand then find out what their favorite beverage of choice is.

- Once the other couple arrives, invite them in and keep the conversation light and friendly. Having some soft music playing in the background can help to keep the conversation flowing. Always be sure to offer your guests a drink (either alcoholic or non-alcoholic) right away and if dinner is not going to be ready shortly then be sure to have light snacks and appetizers ready.

- Make sure you give them rules to follow, as well, while they are in your home. Provide refreshments and light snacks. Play sexy games. Know their boundaries and make sure they know yours.

- It is always wise to be prepared for the other couple to spend the night regardless of what was prearranged, especially if alcoholic beverages are being served. It is never acceptable to send another couple off in a condition that would be dangerous to them.

- If it is against your rules to have the couple sleep in your home then be kind enough to call them a taxi cab, and be prepared to pay for the cab as well. Be sure to help return their vehicle to them the next day. At some point throughout the following week, leave them a note or a message thanking them for their company and the good time.

Hosting a couple is a lot more intimate than hosting a party can be, because it is just the four of you and not a houseful of guests. You can still orchestrate the evening, but the night will move faster than it will with a houseful.

Be aware, however, that swapping with the same couple over and over again has been found to create problems with some couples. If you favor one couple or person over others, you run the risk of falling into infatuation with one or the other. Also, if you are only comfortable swapping with one couple, you will never get to experience anyone else. If they move, you will find you may have burned a few bridges behind you. You have only ever swapped with them, and others in the club may be afraid you will try to single them out as well. If you do want to host a couple, make sure you are taking the time to host other couples sometimes as well.

Being Gracious Guests

- Always respond to an invitation in a timely manner. Be sure to take note of the time of arrival and show up within 5 – 10 minutes of that time. It is very rude to be too early or too late. You could possibly catch the couple not prepared for your arrival yet or even worse show up and be awkwardly standing on their doorstep when they arrive home from the restaurant where they picked up dinner for the night.

Equally as bad, if not worse, is showing up too late or not at all. Often the other couple will have dinner going or ready and waiting for you, and it is extremely rude to make them wait on your arrival. Should something occur at the last minute that keeps you from being able to make it, be sure to pick up the phone and call your hosts to let them know what is going on. But don't be surprised if you do not get a second chance. Swingers and most people in general are not fans of being stood up on the first date, regardless of the reason.

- Be sure to bring your hosts a bottle of wine or some beer to the occasion (or a non-alcoholic beverage if your hosts do not imbibe). It is especially nice if you go out of your way and call to ask if they need you to pick up anything on the way over.

- Know the rules of the house, the rules of the party, and/or the rules of the club. Do not go into any party without familiarizing yourself with these first.

- Do not bring an excessive amount of toys, clothing or jewelry as it can be tedious and embarrassing to have to spend a lot of time packing up or looking for lost things.

- Do not bother the hostess too often. If you have questions, ask another guest. For instance, imagine the party started at six o'clock, and you and your partner did not arrive until seven thirty. You have missed the dinner, but are in time for the games and playing. You are not sure where to put your belongings or where the dress down area is. Ask another guest first. The hostess/host is busy making sure their plans go as they wanted. They may be a bit frazzled; try not to add to it.

- Pick up after yourself. If you have garbage, throw it away. If you brought towels, take them home with you when you leave. If you leave them there, be sure to contact the hosts as soon as possible, or the towels may become an addition to their towel collection.

- Always offer to change the sheets and help clean up with dinner or any other messes that are made.

- Be polite; thank the host and hostess for the party when you arrive. Thank them again when you leave. Remember, you are in someone else's home (or could be responsible for extra fees added to the hotel room), treat it as you would any other person's home—with respect.

- Do not drink so much that you cannot get yourselves home at the end of the night if that was the prearranged plan, and be sure to leave first thing in the morning or immediately after breakfast if you are invited to stay.

- Pay close attention to the behavior and the vibe that you are receiving from both members of the hosting couple, and be sure to never overstay your welcome. Few things are as irritating as the couple that won't take the hint that it is time to go home.

- If they ask for a donation, bring it. You would want everyone to help you out if you were hosting a party, do the same for them. Think about all of the cost and time put into the party. They've spent days getting the party ready. They have prepared their house for their guests. After the party, they have to wash every sheet, blanket, towel, wash cloth, and surface in the house. A donation will go a long way.

- Find out what rooms you can play in and which rooms are off limits. The host and hostess will probably do this at the beginning of the party, but if you show up after they have told everyone what is what, ask other party goers to give you directions.

- If there is a hot tub and it is not open, do not assume that it is ok for you to open it up and take a dip. It may be off limits. It may be that the host or hostess forgot to open it. If you see them around, ask if you can use it or not. Some people do not like to have their hot tubs used because people vary so much with what temperature they like.

They may get complaints that it is too hot and then someone else may complain that it is too cool after they change the temperature. In addition, they have to clean it out after it has been used and may not want to add that chore to all the other ones they will have the next day.

Chapter 5: Swinging Discreetly – How To Swing without Ruining Your Career And Social Reputation

While most people in the swinging lifestyle are happy to be in the lifestyle, they understand that the average citizen does not understand the concept. Other people have preconceived notions of what goes on in the lifestyle and may not have a lot of tolerance for those in the lifestyle. Swingers do not generally want the outside world to know they are part of the lifestyle. Many could suffer should word get out to the wrong person about their personal, extracurricular activities.

So how exactly does one keep their personal identity safe in a world where people post profile pictures and nightclubs let in anyone with a wife/partner?

One way to avoid spilling the proverbial beans is to watch how you speak to them when you are in public, on the phone, or online. A few general rules you can follow are:

- Do not talk about what went on at a party or a swap, even if you know the other person you are speaking to was at the same party you were. Keep your private life and those of the swingers you are with private. It is not anyone else's business what goes on in your bedroom. Ever.

- Do not give out other people's numbers or address to a third party. If someone gave you their number, they gave it to you because they want you to call them and set up a date. They did not give it to you so that other people will call them.

- Never call only the husband or wife of another couple to speak privately or to arrange a private date. This is cheating and is a big no-no in the lifestyle. Doing this will not only ruin your reputation in the real world, but also in your personal life and with people who are in the lifestyle with you. If you are calling another couple, call the couple—speak to the person who answers, but speak to them as part of the couple.

- Give your phone number to someone else if you want them to contact you, but do not expect them to reciprocate. In other words, do not say, "Here's my number, now give me yours." You are putting them in an awkward situation in which they may acquiesce and give you their number, but they may not really want to set up a play date.

- If you call someone and they put you off each time, let it go. It may be that they felt there was a connection at the party, but now they are not really interested in taking things further. Do not keep calling them over and over again. After three tries, give it up. Take the hint. They do not want to play.

- If you do call someone and an answering machine picks up, keep the message short and simple. Do not leave overly sexual messages; you never know who will be listening to them. If you are calling to talk about a party, ask them if they are free to talk first or if you should call them back at a better time. They may have guests or family at the house or their children may be present. Give them the time and the space in which to speak to you when they are comfortable and able to do so. Another good idea here is to be sure that the person you are talking to is the right person. You would not want to be talking to Henry about the upcoming sex party, and then find out that it was Henry, Jr. you were speaking with.

- Unless you know the other couple very well, do not give out your street address. You do not want people to randomly show up looking for swinging partners.

- Do not tell your family about your lifestyle. You may be tempted. It is fun and exciting and you are so happy. You want them to know! But that elation passes and real life asserts itself. No matter how much you love it, they may not understand it, may not want to understand it, and may not want to hear about it anyway. You will regret your revelations, and they will forever look at you differently.

The same goes for online discussions. You may want to post on Facebook or Twitter that you are at a sex party. You may want to publicly thank the host for throwing such an awesome party. Do not. Step away from the keyboard until the desire passes.

Some swinger's clubs even make you sign a nondisclosure agreement (NDA) to make sure you do not "out" any members of the club.

If you swing online, there are some precautions you can make. When you create your profile do not use your real name. You can use something obviously fake and generic, like your dream porn star name or John Smith, Sally Jones, etc. You can also choose to not include the name of your home town, especially if it is a small one. Instead, use the name of the nearest larger town or city.

Ideally, you would put nothing in your profile about yourself that could cause people to narrow things down so that they can tell who you are and where you live. If you are going to post photographs of yourself and your partner be sure to crop off the head or blur it out. Should you be worried about identifying tattoos or piercings then blur those or try to avoid showing them in any photographs as well.

Like you, most swingers wish to maintain a high level of discretion, so it is always best to assume that everyone within the swinging community wishes to keep their sexual behavior private and discreet.

For the discreet couple who wishes to swing in public settings like nightclubs, things can get a bit more difficult. It helps to live near a densely populated city that has a host of Swingers Clubs. These clubs will often hold a night where masks or costumes are involved. These would be the nights to take advantage of.

Being able to go out in a costume which covers your face and makes you unrecognizable, giving you confidence in being able to meet other swingers (without worrying about the guy from floor 3 at the office, who swings with his girlfriend recognizing you!) can add a lot of excitement to your evening.

Perhaps one of the best ways to go about swinging and protecting your identity is to find a group of swingers who are similar to you. Private swinging groups often only interact with the other members of the group. The screening processes are highly rigorous to ensure that there is no conflict of work or interests within the members of the group. They are very discreet and function quietly, but they are out there if you look hard enough.

Another safe way to is to cautiously get to know individual couples via online messaging or Skype before meeting and revealing yourselves to them as a couple.

Be sure that you are 100% comfortable with the energy that you are picking up from the other couple before agreeing to meet with them in real life.

Giving away your true identity only to those you trust. Finding other couples with profiles that are similar to yours is also a way to find others that you know will value your privacy as much as you do.

Discretion is paramount to the swinger community. It is understood that what goes on is not discussed anywhere other than within swinging circles. Promote the lifestyle, but do not publicize it. In other words, it's okay if you or others wish to talk about what a wonderful way it is to live. It is not, however, okay to discuss with your neighbor the variety of sexual positions you accomplished with the two mutual friends who came over to your home last night.

Chapter 6: Exploring Fetishes

You have probably had a lot of exposure to sex in this point in your life, but you may not have. There are a lot of fetishes and kinks out there, both in the swinging world and out of it. Some people are perfectly happy with "normal" sex, while others seek something more. Some people cannot feel sexy unless they do certain acts. Some people, on the other hand, are just interested in trying new things.

A fetish is described by Miriam-Webster as "an object or bodily part whose real or fantasied presence is psychologically necessary for sexual gratification and that is an object of fixation to the extent that it may interfere with complete sexual expression."

In the late 1800's a French psychologist, Alfred Binet, came up with the idea that fetishes can be split into two categories, those that are plastic and those that are spiritual. Spiritual fetishes are those that would be attached to a mental state, social class or economic role. Plastic fetishes would be the ones which are related to specific body parts, clothing, toys or other physical objects.

Swinging itself is a fetish for some, and there are many more fetishes which are openly explored and promoted within the swinging lifestyle. Voyeurism, exhibitionism, cuckolding, bondage, submissive and dominant behavior, spanking, feet, big breasts, tickling and water sports are all fetishes that may be incorporated into swinging. There is pretty much a fetish out there for everyone and those who say they don't have one may be in denial. Let's face it, as swinging can be considered a fetish all of us who engage in it have at least THAT one shared fetish!

A big misconception about swingers is that any sex party is a sex free-for-all, an anything goes extravaganza, but that simply is not true. The type of party depends on the type of participants. Just like making sure your guests are all full or soft swap, it is important for any host or hostess to know or determine what kinks and fetishes will be welcome at the party.

Different kinks and fetishes require different items to ensure they work out well. For instance, a BDSM party will need a lot of restraints and maybe some plastic sheeting. If you have voyeurs and/or exhibitionists at the party, you need to make sure that everyone is ok with that or that you have rooms set aside for them.

Let's take a look at what these different fetishes look like, and how they may be presented. Consider how you will deal with them as a couple regardless whether you've dabbled in some already yourself. Just as with the other elements of swinging, it is important to always maintain an open mind. Allow yourself the opportunity to work out your personal sexual desires and obsessions freely and uninhibitedly. If, after trying out a new fetish, you find that you did not enjoy it, then you know that you will want to exclude it from future engagements.

The important thing to remember is that just because you don't enjoy a particular fetish or activity is not a reason to judge someone else who does. Swinging attracts couples with a wide range of tastes, and one of the tenets of the swinging community is the exploration of new experiences.

You don't have to avoid a couple that you know enjoys a certain fetish just because you don't. If you find the other couple to be attractive to you in other ways, simply invite them to play, but with the understanding that you prefer to leave that fetish out of the equation.

A big misconception about swingers is that any sex party is a sex free-for-all, an anything goes extravaganza, but that simply is not true. The type of party depends on the type of participants. Just like making sure your guests are all full or soft swap, it is important for any host or hostess to know or determine what kinks and fetishes will be welcome at the party. Different kinks and fetishes require different items to ensure they work out well. For instance, a BDSM party will need a lot of restraints and maybe some plastic sheeting. If you have voyeurs and/or exhibitionists at the party, you need to make sure that everyone is ok with that or that you have rooms set aside for them.

Now, in the next few chapters we will take a closer look at some common fetishes you may encounter.

Chapter 7: Voyeurism And Exhibitionism

Voyeurism is the act of observing people performing sexual acts, usually in the context of spying. It can range from someone hiding in the closet and watching you have sex through the slats, to someone sitting in the room while you and your partner are getting it on. It may involve masturbation by the watcher.

Traditionally most voyeurs do not engage with their subjects. Within the swinging community, voyeurism can incorporate the pleasure that one partner receives from watching their partner engage in sexual activities with a fellow swinger, but unlike the traditional concept of a voyeur hiding in the shadows, in this case the voyeurism takes place in the open, with all partners being aware of the element of voyeurism that is present.

At parties and events when men or women are watching others play and interact sexually, they are playing the role of the voyeur if they are becoming aroused and getting sexual gratification from it. Quite often they are. The joy of being a voyeur within the swinger lifestyle is arrived at by watching willing exhibitionists, often times their own partner, and being involved in the experience and also being able to interact with their subject sexually after they watch them with the other lover. Another element of the fetish that many voyeurs in swinging situations find appealing is that often they are even able to join in if it is allowed or requested by the parties playing the exhibitionists.

Exhibitionism is the act of exposing or performing sexual acts in public, usually with a strong desire to be watched or caught. This is seen mostly with couples who enjoy having sex in public areas like restrooms, elevators, or movie theatres. But you can also be an exhibitionist at a party. Just make sure that you let people know it is OK to watch.

Once again, in the swinging lifestyle, quite often the recipient of the actions of the exhibitionist is a willing participant to the exposure. Exhibitionists within the swinging world are the men and women who have no problem making out with their own partner or other partners in front of the whole party or club. Nor do they have any problem going farther than that and having sex with them wildly and passionately in front of others. They get off on the attention and love having the eyes on them as they make love to the other person or persons that they are playing with.

Many men and women enjoy either one or both of the aspects of exhibitionism. While it is more common that most people either being a voyeur OR an exhibitionist, there are many people that enjoy participating in both aspects. It is not uncommon to find a voyeur switching to their exhibitionist side as they are invited to join the group that is playing or to take their turn with the exhibitionist. Thus the voyeur then becomes the exhibitionist.

If a man or woman decides to take a step aside as another member moves in and begins to relax and watch the new group play she has then moved from exhibitionist to voyeur. The joy of being in the swinger lifestyle is that there is freedom to perform and act upon these desires and to have them welcomed by others who understand them.

Not only does that freedom exist, but it is all consensual, which makes it a far more acceptable practice than watching your neighbors have sex through a window! In a swinging situation, there is a happy ending for both the voyeur and the exhibitionist, making the practice of voyeurism and exhibitionism a bit different than the definitions that currently exist as they pertain to the world outside of swinging.

Chapter 8: Cuckolding

Cuckolding is the practice wherein a woman engages in sex with someone other than her partner, and has traditionally applied to circumstances where the husband is not aware that his wife is having sex with other men. A cuckold refers to a man allowing their partner to have sex with different partners.

Outside of swinging circles, as well as within the swinging community, cuckolding is often characterized by a sexually inadequate husband who accepts the fact that his wife is the one who makes the decisions about who she has sex with. It usually involves the female in the relationship to achieve a more dominant role as the male assumes a submissive role. It can have multiple sub-fetishes attached, such as forced feminization to the male, male chastity devices or interracial cuckolding.

Cuckolding is almost exclusively relegated to situations where the man is the partner that is being "cheated on" or being forced to accept the inclusion of another man, or "bull." The cuckold gets sadomasochistic pleasure from the humiliation of being left out or not preferred over the other man. He can also get pleasure from the chance to share or participate in the experience in the form of an open relationship or a swinger relationship. A woman who is engaging in this fetish is often referred to as a *cuckqueen*, or *hotwife* or *slutwife*.

Cuckolding can also be a common practice amongst swinging couples, particularly those who have a partner that travels a lot, leaving the other spouse alone often, allowing for the female partner to have playmates and sexual gratification and entertainment as they see fit while their husbands are gone traveling and working.

Cuckold relationships can work in a variety of ways. Sometimes the women want to sleep with only guys in a different race, as the interracial element is a factor for the cuckolding fetish for many couples. More often than not the men that they are choosing are much better endowed than their husbands, and they are treated as alpha over the husband.

In most cases, the bull is allowed to finish having sex with the woman before the husband is allowed to engage with his wife. Often times this can involve the husband having to orally clean up the cum which is dripping out of the wife left by the new alpha male before he is allowed to begin. If you see the term "Alpha male or bull male wanted" by a couple on a swinging lifestyle site, this is often what it is referring to.

There is also a deviation, though very rare, in which the woman allows the man to have sex with different partners. These women are referred to as cuckqueans. It implies that the watcher is forced to watch the sex play and, in some instances, she is forced to clean up after the sexual activity.

There is a large subculture of cuckolds on the internet. There is poetry and art related to cuckolds and cuckqueans as well as forums, blogs, and groups.

Chapter 9: Dom/sub and BDSM

Dominant/submissive relationships, otherwise known as Dom/sub or D/s can exist in an almost unlimited variety of situations, from monogamous to swinger and polyamorous relationships. Cuckolding is usually considered a form of a Dom/sub relationship.

BDSM is a variety of consensual sexual practices that involve bondage, domination, sadism, and masochism. The play usually revolves heavily around the roles of dominance and submission. Can involve verbal, mental, and physical abuse but should always be practiced with mutual respect for boundaries set by each individual.

Often the submissive partner (or sub) in the relationship will wear a collar which signifies to whom they belong, or who their owner is. Their owner is the dominant partner (or Dom, or Domme if female), who controls the sub by telling them what to do and having them follow various commands or perform various acts. Although on the surface it may seem that the dominant one is in control, quite often it is really the submissive that is ultimately in control, by allowing the dominant one to have control over them and by placing the boundaries on how far the dominant partner is allowed to dominate or push them sexually.

Some of the many variations of a dominant/submissive relationship can include public or private verbal and erotic humiliation and bondage, domestic servitude or consensual slavery, corporal punishment, equestrian themed gear and role playing or other dehumanizing animal play, whipping, spanking, feminization or cross-dressing, gagging, latex and bondage clothing, toys and equipment, binding and tying up, and restricting one from having sex while they are forced to watch the dominant one play. The important factor is that both the submissive and dominant partners are comfortable in their roles.

Bondage is when the other person is tied up, bound, or restrained for erotic purposes. It can be the start of sex, with other BDSM activities, or an end all in itself, depending upon the participant. People can be bound with rope, cuffs, bondage tape, ribbon, bandages, or any type of material that will allow a person to be bound without causing too much damage. Bondage creates a submissive and dominant atmosphere with the bound person becoming the submissive of the knot maker.

Spanking can encompass a whole host of different styles and degrees. It can involve barehanded spanking of body parts or spankings with the use of various equipment such as belts, whips, and paddles. Everyone has different pain thresholds, so parameters or safe words should be utilized, especially when spanking is first being introduced. Some people enjoy spanking and high degrees of pain while others do not tolerate any degree of pain and personal limits should be respected.

There are many wonderful night clubs that are aimed specifically at this fetish. Some offer a more intense experience than others. Research them a bit before you head into one so you can be fully prepared for the night ahead.

It is important when going into such play-dates and experiences that everyone is fully aware of what is going to happen and who is playing what roles. Usually there is an agreement that all parties are open to any acts as long as they are within reasonable and safe limits given the situation and circumstances.

Quite often there are contracts or waivers for all parties to sign which release the Dominant one from any possible legal liabilities they could incur from the injuries which can result from such playing and interaction. There are a variety of different contracts, from slave contracts to scene contracts. Slave contracts tend to be more long term and are traditionally not legally binding but more for show and ritual between the submissive and the dominant partner. Such contracts offer a way of committing themselves to one another within the lifestyle.

When couples engage in a D/s experience, it is often called a *"scene."* Some clubs offer areas that are referred to as *"dungeons."* A dungeon can be anything from a specially designed room, with all manner of toys and apparatus (picture a dungeon scene from a film set is the medieval ages) to a regular room set apart from other areas but meant to contain D/s scenes. Scene contracts or dungeon contracts can be quite simple or very extensive, covering everything from place and duration of play time to actions and behaviors that are allowed in the dungeon and during the agreed upon playtime.

Often times, along with the contract comes the collaring ceremony. These can be done in private or public. Normally within the swinging community, and especially the active Dom/sub community, they are performed publicly and can be held with quite a bit of flair, almost being treated similarly to a wedding of sorts.

The significance of the collar in the Dom/sub lifestyle is very important but not always widely accepted within the more normal non-sexual aspects of society. Some subs opt for wearing a white or skin colored collar, which is less noticeable when they are out and about with their vanilla friends, while others may choose to wear a symbolic bracelet or anklet. Many couples forego the wearing of collars in the vanilla world and reserve their use for when they are engaging in sexual activities. Sometimes the collars are worn in everyday life, but a more elaborate collar is chosen for play times.

Be careful when going out to BDSM clubs as swingers as many clubs are geared toward BDSM and not necessarily swingers too, and it might be easy to confuse the two clubs and assume that both behaviors are welcome when that is not the case. When combining BDSM and swinging, be sure to be very communicative and never ever share your partner unless things have been clearly agreed upon and discussed between both Doms.

It is a common misconception among swingers that the BDSM scene maintains rules similar to their own. This could not be further from the truth. Swingers are those whose first fetish is swapping partners or sharing lovers, while within the BDSM scene, occasionally there is partner swapping or sharing or a little bit of polyamory action, but for the most part the focus remains on the Dom/sub relationship and the actions that are taken within that relationship. The clubs or groups that host either D/s scenes or swingers should make their policies clear. If you are unsure as to the nature of a club, ask!

Being Submissive or Dominant in a Swingers Society

Quite often the lines and themes of submission and dominance are brought easily and happily into the swinger's lifestyle. There are many swingers who consider themselves to be subs or Doms (or even "switches" -- people that enjoy both roles) in the swinger community. Each and everyone one of them has a different and unique way of bringing their two fetishes together.

More often than not the couple who is heavily into BDSM will only lightly incorporate it with their swinging partners, if at all, and only after discussing everything and having an agreement between everyone. Sometimes swinger hosts will have parties or events that are slightly BDSM oriented, but they are more for dressing up and playing the part (such as some light spanking or directing of already willing participants) than they are for actual hard dominance, humiliation, or physical dominant activities.

Not all Dom/sub activities require physical pain, tying or punishment. Many Dom/sub interactions can be based along more mental forms of domination and control as well as subservience. Subs can make their partner happy by performing a number of acts, from chores around the house to dressing the way that they wish them to, to pleasing the other people and partners that they wish them to and in the manner that they wish them to.

Submissive women are almost always allowed to play with the women of their choosing. If they wish to play with other men sexually, they often need to get permission from their dominant partner before performing any acts with the other man. Sometimes if it has been agreed upon beforehand, the submissive partner will happily do the bidding of the dominant one and engage with whomever they are directed at the event or party. Allowing their control to be total, and creating a highly sexually charged environment and scene for the rest of those attending the party can be a large aspect of the D/s element when combined with swinging.

Should the two of you be heavily into BDSM, it would be wise to search out a group or another couple who is into the concept in a similar manner that you both are. If both the women are subs, perhaps discuss the option of trading flat out or taking turns with both of them. It might be a bit difficult to combine two Doms into one sexual encounter but I have seen it done before.

Some people within the Dom/sub world can play the part of the switch, as mentioned earlier. These people tend to be pretty rare, as most find themselves drawn heavily towards one or the other mindset. The switches can be very helpful and convenient when in multiple party settings. Switching to sub when convenient and allowing for one person to be the established Dom within the play group can help "even" things out. They can also switch to Dom when groups of playing people are being more submissively oriented.

Play Rough But Play Safe - How to Take It to the Edge without Taking It Too Far

It is within the nature of the Dominant/submissive relationship for there to be intense situations. These situations often involve binding and gagging, some beating or whipping of sorts, light choking and other forms of physically dominant activity.

Usually, these situations also involve more mentally charged dynamics of domination and humiliation as well, but it is the physical aspects which can cause harm if precautions are not laid out so that the recipient of the actions or punishments is able to stop them should things go far. It is important to know when it is ok to push the line a little bit, and when to stop from going too far, maintaining a balance of excitement and pleasure as well as safety for everyone.

Since quite often it is part of the game or act that is going on for the submissive to resist or react in a negative manner to the pain or punishment, it is crucial that a safety word be designated for the submissive one to call out should things begin to get too intense for them. Safety words are often made of silly nonsensical simple words like "whale" or "penguin." It is wise to not make this word something that would be normally said during these situations such as "no" or "stop."

What To Do If The Safe Word Is Called

The Dom needs to cease all play immediately if the safe word is called. Then follow that by taking the time to sit down and discuss with the offended sub the infraction in a calm, sensitive and understanding manner. Discussing limits beforehand will ideally prevent this from happening. But sometimes it still does, and when it does be sure to talk to the sub until they are feeling 100% better and safe within the situation again. Be sure to not push the limits to where they need to use the safe word again.

In addition to a safety word it is a good idea to add a pair of safety scissors or EMT shears to your kit. Ones that can cut through ANYTHING, just in case you have an emergency, can't get ropes untied, or start to have panic attack from being bound too tightly, or feeling too constricted to breath.

While it is easy to get carried away with the fantasies of a Dom/sub relationship, it is important to keep your actions and treatments sane. DO not go overboard or take things too far. There is a big difference between fantasizing about beating someone with a whip made of barbed wire; it is a whole other level to go through with such thoughts in real life. Keep your actions and thoughts realistic and sane within the lifestyle.

A healthy and productive Dom/sub relationship relies on the three corner stones: **trust, safety and surrender**.

The trust should already be established in a healthy and honest swinging relationship as respect and boundaries between different couples are also established. If there is to be a successful combination of swinging and D/s, it is of utmost importance to have established that trust before attempting to bring the Dominant/submissive thought process and ideas to the swinger lifestyle. The couple or partner that you are bringing in to your ways of playing must be able to trust that you will not go too far with them, and vice versa depending on who is being the dominant one.

Safety is the second corner stone. The submissive must not only feel safe but they must know that they ARE safe, and without this trust and establishment of security it is impossible for the relationship or games to continue on and be enjoyed by the submissive. Both the submissive and the dominant partners must make sure the communication is healthy and clear, so that no boundaries are crossed which make the submissive feel unsafe or in danger.

Surrender is the third corner stone of the healthy Dom/sub relationship, and will come easily once the first two are in place. Together they make up a healthy working Dom/sub relationship and should be applied to interactions with other couples that you invite to play with you within the lifestyle.

Aftercare is another important part of Dom/sub relationship, and should also be prepared for in your kit. Bring Band-Aids and antiseptic if you might be participating in activities which would cause minor injuries. Be prepared to spend time after the activity with the subs, nursing them and being sweet to them, both physically and mentally.

Avoid playing with other couples that are in an abusive or unhealthy Dom/sub relationship as well. A good Dom will work to have a proud and happy sub, while the abusive ones get off on having sad ones that are always doing wrong or needing to be punished. Abusive Doms will constantly work to create situations in which their sub cannot or is not performing up to par, thus allowing them to constantly belittle and berate them.

Lack of prior set limits or safe words are other great warning signs of unhealthy sub/Dom relationships to avoid. Isolation, dependency and having a Dom who is quick to anger are other signs of an off balance relationship you will wish to steer clear of.

As a good Dom, if you are allowing your sub to play away from your company with another Dom and subs, it is your responsibility to participate in the making sure that everything is okay. Both partners should contribute to assuring the other that the scenes are appropriate to the couple's parameters, and maintain excellent communication before, during and after play.

Chapter 10: Tickling and Other Lighter Fetishes

There are a variety of different lighter fetishes which you may encounter in the swinging world that are less known about and encountered. Everything from foot fetishes and belly buttons to smoking, aliens, tickling, fire, wax, ice and age play.

Some people and couples have fetishes which compel them to being attracted to certain races or looks of people, like Asians, blacks, blonds, redheads, men with beards, heavy men, and women with large breasts or women with little ones. There are people with fetishes centered on butts, tattoos, piercings and crazy hair. Finger nails and lipstick, braids, pigtails and ponytails are other fetishes centered on the human appearance. The wearing of high heels, lingerie and corsets, thigh highs, miniskirts, school girl skirts can all be a fetish as well.

Pretty much anything you can think of that would cause sexual attraction or arousal for someone can be a fetish.

Tickling Fetish – Everyone knows what tickling is and everyone has been tickled. However, the fetish of tickling goes beyond the childish play that most people think of when they think of tickling. A lot of tickling is done using items such as feathers, forks, or anything really. Some ticklers prefer to bind their partner so that they cannot wiggle out of the tickling. Some do not. Some tickle for a few minutes before sex play, and some tickle for forty minutes or so.

There are the ticklers who love to watch their partner squirm, giggle, and beg for them to stop. They derive a certain sexual satisfaction out of watching the effects of their tickling. Then there are the ticklees, those who love to laugh, love the feeling of being tickled. Since tickling releases endorphins, our "happy hormones," into our system, this makes a lot of sense.

The tickling can wind down, after the first throes of giggling, into something more intimate. It can travel down to the pubic area, where the giggling can stop and the moaning can start. However, as mentioned before, just because you like being tickled does not mean you have a tickling fetish. It becomes a fetish when you derive sexual pleasure from it.

Some other lighter fetishes include, but are not limited to:

- **Sex either fully or partially clothed** – both partners are either partially or fully clothed. This is also referred to as *dry humping*.

- **Fingers in the mouth** – this is the simple act of someone either sucking on their own fingers, sucking on another person's fingers, or making someone suck on their fingers.

- **Orgasm denial** – this is having sex or masturbating until you are just about ready to come and then you stop. You deny it. Or it is having sex, oral sex, or masturbating the other person and watching their reactions and not allowing them to cum.

- **Inexperienced partners** – this is a fetish that involves either the real thing (actual inexperienced partners) or role-playing that one of them is not experienced with sexual intercourse. This stems from the idea that teaching someone how to have sex is hot. Being taught how to have sex is pretty darn hot as well.

- **Videography** – making videos of the sex play. This is not something you would see a lot at a swinger's gathering, since taking pictures is not something most swingers want you to do.

- **Breast play** – having someone play with your breasts or having someone watch while you play with your breasts.

- **Story driven role-play** – this is a type of role-play that is so in-depth it is almost like making a movie or starring in a play. It goes behind simple characters, fleshing them out and making them "real." These story driven role-plays can be long-term and usually are. The stories you act out can range from pregnancy, birth, science fiction (alien invasion, aliens impregnating women, space sex) to historical re-enactment and everything in between.

- **Shaving** – this is the act of either partner shaving the other or watching while you shave yourself or someone else shaves you. This is usually shaving in the genital region, but can include shaving the legs, face, or armpits.

Pictophilia is the fetish of having a fascination with pornographic pictures. Media fetishes incorporate materials such as leather, latex, silk, rubber, vinyl or feathers. Water can be an amazing fetish for many, enjoying sex in the shower, bath tub, hot tub, swimming pool, oceans, and lakes and even in rain and thunderstorms. Some people prefer older men and women while others have fetishes for the younger crowd.

Chapter 11: Water Sports and More Taboo Fetishes

There is a darker side of fetishes, but very rarely does it rear its head within the swinger's world. Should you happen to encounter one of these and they, like most normal people, leave you cringing and wishing you had never heard of them, then by all means feel free to exercise a firm "NO" and leave to find something more suitable to your tastes and preferences.

- **Water Sports**, or **Bathroom Activities**, have a number of different terms, such as golden showers, scat, brown showers, and salirophilia, and these are fetishes that revolve around urinating or defecating on another person during the act of sex. It can take as simple of a form as one partner peeing or defecating on the other partner's body, to doing so in their mouth. Sometimes the receiving partner also engages in playing with the poo or rubbing it on their body. The thought of which is horrifying and terrifying to most. In addition, there is a higher incidence of being able to transmit various disease and pathogens with feces than with other kinks. A well-known video involving scat play is called *Two Girls, One Cup*.

- **Adult Breast Feeding (ABR)**: Usually involves a lactating woman, but can also be completely role-play in nature. When a woman is lactating her partner will suckle at her breasts just as a baby would. This can be done even if the woman is not lactating at the time. That is where the role-play comes in. The suckling partner can or may also be into infantilism.

- **Age Play**: A type of fetish which involves role-playing either someone significantly older or younger than they are. This can also be someone who is pretending or role-playing to be either very young or older than the other person. For example, a woman may dress up as a school girl, and the man may dress up as a professor. **Pedophelia** is when the fetish revolves around sexual acts with little kids. This is **NOT okay** to participate in on any level. Any attempt to engage in this fetish is not only immoral, but also illegal.

- **Anal/Painal**: Having anal sex with your partner. Painal is when you have anal sex with the intent of causing pain to your partner. The partner in this scenario actually derives pleasure from the pain. Most swingers' clubs frown on anal with strangers because it is one of the most harmful sexual positions. This does not mean that you cannot have anal sex whilst at a party, it just means you should know the person well.

- **Asphyxiation Play**: The act of choking, smothering, or strangling someone during sex either with your hands or other body parts, such as your buttocks or breasts. Always be sure you know the safe word or gesture that tells you when to stop.

- **Breeding or Impregnation Fetish**: Involves a fetish for impregnating your sex partner or having others impregnate your partner. This is usually involved in the cuckolding world, as the thought that the other man may get their wife pregnant turns them on. It can also refer to women who are turned on by the thought of someone impregnating them.

- **Bukkake**: Involves a group of men masturbating or receiving oral or manual sex and ejaculating over a single woman, usually on her face or body.

- **Cream Pie Fetish**: Can involve one or multiple partners in which the person or group of people ejaculate into the vagina or anus, which then oozes out like a creamy pie.

- **Fat Admirer/Worshipper**: A fetish involving obesity in which a person finds another person sexually attractive the more weight they gain. It has several sub-fetishes such as feedism, which involves sex while consuming food of some sort.

- **Foot Fetish**: A common fetish of a non-sexual object such as the foot. It can encompass being sexually excited by feet, shoes, socks or stocking. Usually involves the fondling of the feet and can sometimes be integrated into sex by using the feet as a vessel for the penis for masturbation or using the foot to penetrate the woman.

- **Furries**: Sexual acts performed by people dressed in furry animal costumes. Sometimes they make love taking the costume off and leaving on the giant heads of the costumes.

  Furries usually have their own community and culture, just as swingers do, but that does not mean that a furry cannot also be a swinger. Some furries purchase their costumes, while some make their own. Do not rent a costume for sex play as others will be wearing it later, and we do not know how well they are cleaned.

- **Gangbangs**: Group sex usually involving one woman and multiple men having sex with her. The sex can involve multiple men simultaneously having sex with the woman using different orifices, or can involve having sex with the woman one male at a time but back to back. The latter version is also referred to as a train.

- **Infantilism**: Also known as adult baby fetish in which one partner regresses to an infant state, often wearing infant clothing or diapers and acting like an infant while another person nurtures and takes care of their every need such as you would with an infant.

- **Orgies**: Similar to gangbangs but usually involves multiple people having sex simultaneously as opposed to one woman and multiple men.

  Orgies are not as common in the swinging community as the media may have led you to believe. However, there are usually open rooms in which group play is encouraged.

- **Rubber/Latex Fetish** : Relates to those individuals that gain sexual enjoyment or excitement by wearing or having their partners wear rubber or latex clothing. The excitement can be due to the smell of rubber or latex, the tactile feel of the materials or the titillating visual input of how the material looks on your partner.

- **Sexual Role-Play**: Involves two or more people acting out different roles in a sexual scenario. It could be just about anything such as teacher and student, prostitute and John, nurse and patient.

While it is okay to explore some sexual fantasies and desires, certain fetishes are 100% unacceptable in any swinger situation. Obvious NOs are murder fetishes, cannibalism fetishes, rape, bug chasers (or people who are attempting to contract HIV or another STD), necrophilia, pedophilia, and bestiality.

Should you be into some of the other legal and yet very strange fetishes, you might find it more difficult to find a group tailored to your needs. Try to find other people who express interest in the same thing that you do to avoid extremely uncomfortable situations for the other swingers around you.

If you happen to find yourself in a situation where one of these odd fetishes is being engaged in around you and you are uncomfortable, always say no and remove yourself from the situation immediately.

Conclusion

Now you have more knowledge under your belt and are ready to further explore your sexuality and the swinging lifestyle. You have learned how important your reputation is for the swinging lifestyle and for the clubs in the swinging lifestyle. To find online clubs and dating sites built for the swinging community, check out the list at the end of the resources section.

You now know how important personal hygiene is to a swinger and the swinging community. You understand that being clean is not just about smelling nice for your encounters, but it is mostly about not spreading disease or causing infections.

You have learned a handful of ethics in which to practice both privately and publicly when you are part of the lifestyle. You know how to behave at a party or in public when you are part of the swinging community. You understand that there are rules in which you have to comply and that some people do not want their private life to become a part of their public life. Through use of good ethics as a couple and as individuals, we can ensure that good times are had by all and allow for maximum benefits and pleasure of both couples.

Do not be judgmental or discriminate, always being open-minded and kind even when something is not for you. Good ethics are the backbone of a good reputation. Work together to uphold each other and allow for easy and quick maneuvering through unwanted or unplanned situations that can occur.

You have discovered how to host a party or couple and be a good guest, all while learning how to swing discreetly. Always be prompt and arrive when you say are going to and never without your partner. Use your social graces as often as possible, and with as many people as possible and regardless of whether you are the host or being hosted, be sure to put the same amount of effort into being polite and respectful of the other parties.

You are ready to play rough, but safely, and have explored different fetishes and kinks. You are ready to get out there and be a part of the lifestyle. Discover amazing scenes such as the BDSM lifestyle has to offer, which can enhance your relationship in both physical and mental ways, allowing for a different interaction within the traditional male/female role. You know that these fetishes and kinks are normal and, thankfully, you can explore your new found kink or fetish with other like-minded individuals or couples without feeling discriminated in any way.

You are now able to explore yourself, both emotionally and physically, to better understand your desires and the swinging community. You know that you need to set up ground "rules" for you and your partner before you swing. You need signals that mean yes, no, or let us get out of here! You understand that you have to take the time to know yourself and your partner before embarking on this journey. Explore your sexuality, explore the lifestyle, and have fun.

It is normal for fantasies to adapt and change as one explores the many different aspects of living a full open sex life with their partner. The key is to be respectful and communicative at all times, of your partner first and foremost, followed by respect for the swingers around you. By being equipped with the "how to" of social etiquette as well as having a thorough run down of the various types of things you may encounter as you begin to discover this wide, unmapped sexual territory together, you are guaranteeing a safe and good time for you and your partner.

I have included a glossary of commonly used terms for swinging, sexual play, fetishes, and kinks. There is also a list, after that, of the abbreviations commonly found in online ads or dating sites.

Don't forget to check out the advanced guide of this series. In the Advanced guide, you will learn:

- Games for two swinging couples

- Games for more than four

- Fun positions for 2 couples (and 3...)

- Starting your own Swingers Club/Adult Lifestyle Group

- Throwing successful swingers parties and special events

- How to successfully bring in another party into a 2-person relationship

- Putting out ads for other couples

- Going on a swingers vacations

- Building a "sucsexful" playroom

- And more...

Happy swinging!

Glossary – Terms, Kinks, and Fetishes

Adult Breast Feeding (ABR): Usually involves a lactating woman but can also be completely role-play in nature.

Age Play: A type of fetish which involves role-playing either someone significantly older or younger than they are.

Air-Tight: One step past double penetration, where the woman also has a cock in her mouth.

Alphas: Can refer to both male and female although usually used in the context of a male. Alphas are the dominant personality within a group.

Anal Sex Terms: "Greek", "the backdoor", "Brown eye", "corn hole", "asshole", "Black Cherry"

Anal Sex: The act of a penis or toy penetrating and fucking one's anus.

Anal/Painal: Anal is having anal sex with your partner. Painal is when you have anal sex with the intent of causing pain to your partner. The partner in this scenario actually derives pleasure from the pain.

Asphyxiation Play: The act of choking or strangling someone during sex, either with your hands or other body parts, such as your buttocks or breasts.

Bareback: Having sex without the protection of a condom.

Betas: Can refer to both male and female, although usually used in the context of a male. Betas are the submissive personality within a group.

Bi-comfortable: A person who is comfortable being around another person who is bisexual, and open to participating in multi–person group sex, although not comfortable giving oral sex, having sex with, or kissing people of the same sex. Some bi-comfortable people are comfortable receiving sexual attention from the same sex but not with giving it. Be sure to clarify before entering into the bedroom with them.

Bi-couple: This is a couple in which both partners are bisexual.

Bisexual: A person who enjoys sexual contact with both sexes. Such a person can also be referred to as bi, "goes both ways," or AC/DC.

Blood sports: Sexual activities that involve the breaking of skin and blood. People involved in blood sports usually use shallow cuts or abrasions to do so. Requires a good amount of trust between partners and can be considered a risky activity due to pathogens in the blood.

Body Painting: A favorite amongst many groups of swingers. Involves the painting of the body with body-safe paints. Can often be used as an icebreaker or party game in groups.

Bottom: A person who is submissive in a relationship. Also refers to homosexual relationships in which the bottom is the submissive or the receiving partner in the sexual act.

Breeding or Impregnation Fetish: Involves a fetish for impregnating your sex partner or having others impregnate your partner. It does not necessarily mean that your partner (or you) are actually getting pregnant, but that the chance is there to become pregnant. People involved in this fetish usually go bareback.

Brown Showers or Scat Play: Similar to golden showers except it involves the use of feces instead of urine. Many of the same principles apply in terms of mess containment and clean up. However, there is a higher incidence of being able to transmit various disease and pathogens with feces than with other kinks.

Bukkake: Involves a group of men masturbating or receiving oral or manual sex and ejaculating over a single woman, usually on her face or body.

Bull: Common term in swinging and cuckolding which refers to a male with a very large penis.

Butt Plugs: Dildo-like insert that can be used to enhance anal sex or prepare the anus for anal sex by stretching the muscles. They come in different shapes and sizes and some come in kits with differing sizes so that you can slowly stretch out the anus muscles.

Cataracts of the Nile: The woman lies on her back with her legs spread. The man with a flaccid or semi-flaccid penis kneels between her thighs and forcefully urinates on her clitoris. The woman should be highly aroused or masturbating to achieve the most gratification while being urinated on.

Chastity devices: These are devices that are used to prevent sexual intercourse. They are available for men and women. Often used in the cuckolding fetish to prevent sexual gratification by the cuckold or cuckquean.

Chubby Chaser: A term that can be applied to both men and women who are sexually attracted to obese partners.

Closed Swinging: Closed swinging occurs when the partners of each couple swap and have sex in separate beds and rooms, often with closed doors. This is also referred to as different-room swap.

Cock Rings: This is a sexual aid which involves a ring around the shaft of the penis in order to sustain an erection. They can come in different materials and sizes and can also be used in conjunction with other rings around the scrotum. Flexible rings are usually favored because they can be easily removed.

Cream Pie Fetish: Can involve one or multiple partners in which the person or group of people ejaculate into the uterus or anus.

Cuckold: A cuckold is the term for a man whose wife is having sex with other partners. This is also a form of submission. It is often done in from of the man, but not always.

Cuckquean: This is a woman cuckold. A cuckold is someone who enjoys watching their partner have sex with other people, but does not necessarily have sex with other people as well.

Double Penetration: Double Penetration occurs when the woman has both her vagina and asshole filled by either two cocks, two toys, or one of both. Double Penetration can be administered by men or women or with toys.

Fat Admirer/Worshipper: A fetish involving obesity in which a person finds another person sexually attractive the more weight they gain. It has several sub-fetishes such as

Feedism: A fetish which involves sex with a consumption of a food element. For instance, a fat man being fed cake by his partner, who is sexually aroused watching him eat the cake.

Foot Fetish: A common kink of a non-sexual object such as the foot. It can encompass being sexually excited by feet, shoes, socks or stockings. Usually involves the fondling of the feet and can sometimes be integrated into sex by using the feet as a vessel for the penis for masturbation or using the foot to penetrate the woman.

French: This term is often used to refer to oral sex, but can be used to describe the style of kissing as well.

Full Swap: A full swap occurs when two couples (at least) switch partners for the purpose of sex. This can include oral only, full penetration, or both, depending on the limits of all involved.

Furries: Sexual acts performed by people dressed in furry animal costumes.

Gangbangs: Group sex usually involving one woman and multiple men having sex. The sex can involve multiple men simultaneously having sex with the woman using different orifices or can involve having sex with the woman one male at a time but back to back.

Glory-holes: This is usually a door or wall with a hole that is large enough for a penis to fit through. Usually used for anonymous oral sex, but can also be used for penetration. It is popular with gay culture, but it has been adopted by swingers and couples.

Golden Showers: The act of urinating on a partner for the purpose of sexual gratification. Various different methods can be used and mess control is very important. Most individuals use plastic sheeting or plastic mattress protectors.

Hedonism: Usually refers to a lifestyle whose primary goal is the experience of pleasure and gratification.

Incest Fetish: Refers to role-playing a familial relationship without actually being related. Such as a daddy-daughter or mother/son role-play during sex.

Infantilism: Also known as adult baby fetish in which one partner regresses to an infant state, often wearing infant clothing or diapers and acting like an infant while another person nurtures and takes care of their every need such as you would with an infant.

Log in the Amazon: The male lies on his back while the partner squats over his penis and manually stimulates it. When the man is about to ejaculate his partner pees forcefully onto his penis moving the stream of urine down and around the length of his penis.

Musical Beds: Usually a party game in the swinging world in which a room with multiple beds is used. Lights are usually off when it starts but each couple starts in their own bed. An external cue such as a bell is used and when the cue goes off the men switch to another bed and have sex with that woman. The lights are usually turned on momentarily so that you can see who your new partner was.

Off-Site Clubs: An off-site club or event is one that does not allow public sexual relations. The couples who wish to interact intimately with each other must arrange for such events to take place off premise at their own home, hotel room, or other agreed upon meeting place.

On-Site Clubs: An on-site club or party is one that allows sexual intercourse and public displays of affection. Some events allow for public playing, while others have rooms set aside for more intimate relations to be had separately.

Open Swinging: The partners swap with all four people on the same bed or in the same room during the sex and playtime.

Orgies: Similar to gangbangs but usually involves multiple people having sex simultaneously as opposed to one woman and multiple men.

Orgy: An orgy is sex between multiple partners or more than four people simultaneously. It is also referred to as "Roman" from time to time, as the Romans were known to have been very promiscuous and comfortable with group sex.

Pansexual: Is the emotional or sexual attraction toward people of any gender or gender identity. In essence they are gender blind and gender is an insignificant aspect of their attraction.

Permission Slips and Hall Passes: Permission slips and hall passes are granted to one half or both halves of the couple when one of the partners is going to be away from the other. The parameters of the passes can vary from couple to couple. These usually allow the holder of the hall pass or permission slip to have intimate relations with someone else while they are away.

Playtime or Playing: Playtime or playing refers to having sex or foreplay.

Polyamory: Is the practice or acceptance of intimate relationships or sexual relationships that are not exclusive in nature. For instance, a polyamorous couple may allow for their partners to indulge in sexual acts with other people outside of their relationship or invite others into their relationship without reprisals. Knowledge and consent is a requirement from everyone involved.

Polysexual: Is the attraction to multiple types of sexuality and is sometimes used synonymously with bi-sexual. However, comparison to bisexuality is frowned upon by people who consider themselves polysexual, as it is reinforces the gender dichotomy that is associated with heterosexuality and homosexuality.

Rape Fetish: The act of pretending to rape your partner. Can involve a simple forced sex scenario or involve mock breaking in and assaulting your partner. All of this is with the explicit consent of both individuals and should involve safety words and respect for boundaries.

Rubber/Latex Fetish: Relates to those individuals that gain sexual enjoyment or excitement by wearing or having their partners wear rubber or latex clothing. The excitement can be due to the smell of rubber or latex, the tactile feel of the materials or the titillating visual input of how the material looks on your partner.

Sexual Role-Play: Involves two or more people acting out different roles in a sexual scenario. It could be just about anything such as teacher and student, prostitute and John, nurse and patient.

Soft Swap: Having sex with another couple in the room, but usually there is no swapping of partners. If there is a swapping, it may entail oral sex only, or some other activity that is short of actual penetration.

Switch or Switch-Hitter: Commonly a term used in BDSM to describe a person who enjoys being the top or bottom and an alternate comfortably between roles of submission and domination.

Top: A person who is dominant in a relationship. Also refers to homosexual relationships in which the top is the dominant or the giving partner in the sexual act.

Vanilla: In a swinger's world, Vanilla refers to couples who do not swing, and people who are not in the lifestyle or have yet become introduced fully to it. It can also be the antithesis of "kinky". In some circles this is a derogatory term.

Commonly Used Acronyms

These acronyms can be found in personal ads, on Craig's List, or used in online dating sites.

420: Seen in ads or personals, commonly refers to pot. For instance 420 friendly means that it is okay for you to use pot around them.

AC/DC: This is another way to say someone is bisexual.

B&D: Bondage & Discipline, which includes discipline and power games and roles, as well as binding and restricting a person during sexual play.

BBC: Seen in ads or personals, commonly refers to Big Black Cock and is a term that usually references interracial sex.

FBSM: Acronym that stands for Full Body Sensual Massage. Can also be Full Body Sexual Massage.

BBW: Big Beautiful Woman (or women) and can sometimes mean Big Black Woman.

BDSM: The fetish of Bondage, Discipline and Sadomasochism. Very similar to B&D, it includes the aspect of deriving sexual pleasure from pain, as well as being disciplined and tied up and bound.

BiF: Seen in ads or personals, commonly refers to Bisexual Female.

BiWM: Seen in ads or personals, commonly refers to Bisexual White Males.

MBM: Seen in ads or personals, commonly refers to Married Black Males.

GHM: Seen in ads or personals, commonly refers to Gay Hispanic Male.

DWF: Seen in ads or personals, commonly refers to Divorced White Female.

C2C: C2C stands for Cam to Cam and is important to know for when other couples want to cam chat with you. This is a very fun and erotic experience, and a great way to feel out your compatibility with another couple, especially for new swingers.

DAP: Double anal penetration.

DDF: Seen in ads or personals, commonly refers to drug/disease free.

DP: Double Penetration.

DTF: Seen in ads or personals, commonly stands for Down To Fuck.

DVP: Double vaginal penetration.

FTM: Seen in ads or personals, commonly refers to a female who is in the process of becoming a male.

FWB: Seen in ads or personals, commonly refers to Friends with Benefits.

HWP: Seen in ads or personals, commonly refers to Height Weight proportionate.

LTR: Seen in ads or personals, commonly refers to Long Term Relationships

M4T: Seen in ads or personals, commonly refers to man for transsexual.

M4W: Seen in ads or personals, commonly refers to man for woman.

MFM: Seen in ads or personals, commonly refers to two heterosexual males and one female.

MMF: Seen in ads or personals, commonly refers to two bi-sexual males and one female.

MW4M: Seen in ads or personals, commonly refers to a man and woman looking for another man to join in.

MW4MW: Seen in ads or personals, commonly refers to a man and woman looking for a man and woman to join in.

PNP: Seen in ads or personals, commonly refers to party n' play which stands for having sex while on drugs. It is not usually associated with marijuana, such as 420 friendly, but with harder drugs, such as cocaine or meth.

SAF: Seen in ads or personals, commonly refers to Single Asian Females.

SO: Seen in ads or personals, commonly refers to Significant Other.

NSA: No Strings Attached or sex with no emotional or relationship attachments wanted.

SSBBW: Stands for super-sized big beautiful woman.

Strap-on: Seen in ads or personals, commonly refers to a woman using a fake strap-on dildo.

Fisting: putting the whole fist into someone's vagina or anal orifice as part of sex.

Sugar daddy/mommy: someone financially supporting another's lifestyle.

TG: Seen in ads or personals, commonly refers to someone who is transgendered.

MW4W: Seen in ads or personals, commonly refers to a man and woman looking for a woman to join in.

Made in the USA
Coppell, TX
09 January 2024

27475586R10075